to cheryl

Happy 7th Birthday

Love from Katie

First published in 1985
by Kingfisher Books Limited
Elsley Court,
20–22 Great Titchfield Street
London W1P 7AD
A Grisewood & Dempsey Company

Reprinted 1986

© Kingfisher Books Limited 1985

BRITISH LIBRARY CATALOGUING
IN PUBLICATION DATA
The Kingfisher Christmas book.
1. Christmas – Literary collections
2. English literature
I. Royds, Caroline
820.8'033 PR1111.C53
ISBN 0 86272 153 9

Design by Philippa Bramson
Photoset by Waveney Typesetters, Norwich
Printed in Italy

To Anna and Saskia, Happy Christmas

For permission to reproduce copyright material
acknowledgement and thanks are due to the following:

Faber & Faber Ltd for two stories by Alison Uttley:
The Christmas Box from "The Adventures
of Sam Pig" and *The Fairy Ship* from "John Barleycorn".
David Higham Associates, J. M. Dent & Sons Ltd, and New
Directions Publishing Corporation, New York, for *Mrs
Prothero and the Firemen*, an extract from "A Child's
Christmas in Wales" by Dylan Thomas.
David Higham Associates and Michael
Joseph Ltd for *Keeping Christmas* from
"Silver Sand and Snow" by Eleanor Farjeon.
Andre Deutsch Ltd for *Don't Tell* from
"Don't put Mustard in the Custard" by Mike Rosen.
Andre Deutsch Ltd for *Early on Christmas Morning*,
an extract from "The Rifle House Friends"
by Lois Lamplugh.
Miss D. E. Collins and J. M. Dent & Sons Ltd
for *A Christmas Carol* by G. K. Chesterton from
"The Collected Poems of G. K. Chesterton".
Oxford University Press for *The Stones
of Plouhinec* from "French Legends, Tales &
Fairy Stories" by Barbara Leonie Picard.
Chappell Music for *The Three Drovers* by John Wheeler.
While every effort has been made to obtain
permission, there may still be cases in which we
have failed to trace a copyright holder, and we
would like to apologize for any apparent negligence.

Other stories in this book are retold from
traditional sources and in this version
are © Kingfisher Books Ltd. *The Nutcracker,
Brer Rabbit's Christmas, A Very Big Cat,
Baboushka* and *The Christmas Story* are retold by
Nora Clarke; *The Little Fir Tree* is by Alison Carter.

KINGFISHER

CHRISTMAS BOOK

A collection of stories,
poems and carols for the
twelve days of Christmas

Selected by Caroline Royds
Pictures by
Annabel Spenceley

KINGFISHER BOOKS

CONTENTS

THE CHRISTMAS BOX

In a small thatched cottage near the edge of the forest lived four young pigs – Tom, Bill, Ann and Sam, and with them, for much of the year, was their guardian Brock the Badger. The little pigs loved dear, kind Brock, and they looked up to him because of his strength and courage and because of his great wisdom.

Winter had come early. By December the pond was frozen solid and the snow lay deep. Every morning when he awoke Sam Pig thought about Christmas Day. He looked at the snow, and he shivered a little as he pulled on his little trousers and ran downstairs. But the kitchen was warm and bright and a big fire burned in the hearth. Tom cooked the porridge and Ann set the table with spoons and plates, and Bill ran out to sweep the path or to find a log for the fire.

After breakfast Sam fed the birds. They came flying down from the woods, hundreds of them, fluttering and crying and stamping their tiny feet, and flapping their slender wings. The big birds – the green woodpeckers, the blue-spangled jays, the dusky rooks and the speckled thrushes – ate from large earthen dishes and stone troughs which Sam filled with scraps. They were always so hungry that the little birds got no chance, so Sam had a special breakfast table for robins and tom tits, for wrens and chaffinches. On a long flat stone were ranged rows of

little polished bowls filled with crumbs and savouries. The bowls were walnut-shells, and every bird had its own tiny brown nutshell.

After the bird-feeding Sam went out on his sledge. Sometimes Bill and Tom and Ann rode with him. Badger had made the sledge, but he never rode on it himself. He was too old and dignified, but he enjoyed watching the four pigs career down the field and roll in a heap at the bottom.

"Good old Badger," thought Sam. "I will give him a nice Christmas present this year. I'll make him something to take back to his house in the woods when he goes for his winter sleep."

That was as far as Sam got. Ann was busy knitting a muffler for Badger. It was made of black and white sheep's wool, striped to match Badger's striped head. Bill the gardener was tending a blue hyacinth which he kept hidden in the wood-shed. Tom the cook had made a cake for Brock. It was stuffed with currants and cherries and almonds as well as many other things like honey-comb and ants' eggs. Only young Sam had nothing at all.

There was plenty of time to make a present, he told himself carelessly, and he swept up the snow from the path and collected the small birds' walnut-shells.

"Christmas is coming," said a robin brightly. "Have you got your Christmas cards ready, Sam?"

"Christmas cards?" said Sam. "What's that?"

"You don't know what a Christmas card is? Why, I'm part of a Christmas card! You won't have a good Christmas without a few cards, Sam."

Sam went back to the house where Ann sat by the fire knitting Badger's muffler. She used a pair of holly-wood knitting needles which Sam had made. A pile of scarlet holly-berries lay in a bowl by her side and she knitted a berry into the wool for ornament here and there.

10

Sam sat down by her side and took up the ball of wool.

"Can I make a Christmas card for Badger?" he asked.

Ann pondered this for a time, and her little needles clicked in tune with her thoughts.

"Yes, I think you can," said she at last. "I had forgotten what a Christmas card was like. Now I remember. There is a paintbox in the kitchen drawer, very, very old. It belonged to our grandmother. She used to collect colours from the flowers and she kept them in a box. Go and look for it, Sam."

Sam went to the drawer and turned over the odd collection of things. There were cough-lozenges and candle-ends, and bits of string, and a bunch of rusty keys, a piece of soap and a pencil, all stuck together with gum from the larch-trees. Then, at the back, buried under dead leaves and dried moss he found the little paintbox.

11

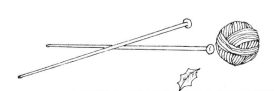

"Here it is! Oh Ann! How exciting," cried Sam, and he carried it to the table.

"It's very dry and the paints all look the same colour," said Ann, "but with a good wash they'll be all right."

"It's a very nice box of paints," said Sam, and he licked each paint carefully with his pointed tongue.

"They taste delicious," said he, smacking his lips. "The colours are all different underneath, and the tastes are like the colours. Look, Ann! Here's red, and here's green and here's blue, all underneath this browny colour."

He held out the box of licked paints which were now gaily coloured.

"The red tastes of tomatoes and the green of wood-sorrel and the blue of forget-me-nots," said Sam.

Badger was much interested in the paintbox when he came in.

"You will want a paint-brush," said he. "You can't use the besom-brush, or the scrubbing-brush, or even your tooth-brush to paint a Christmas card, Sam."

Badger plucked a few hairs from his tail and bound them together.

"Here! A badger-brush will be excellent, Sam."

"What shall I have to paint on?" asked Sam, as he sucked the little brush to a point and rubbed it on one of the paints.

That puzzled everybody. There was no paper at all. They looked high and low, but it wasn't till Tom was cooking the supper that they found the right thing. Tom cracked some eggs and threw the shells in the corner. Sam took one up and used the badger-brush upon it.

"This is what I will have," he cried, and indeed it was perfect, so smooth and delicate. Bill cut the edges neatly and Sam practised his painting upon it, making curves and flourishes.

"That isn't like a Christmas card," said Ann, leaning over his

12

shoulder. "A Christmas card must have a robin on it."

"You must ask the robin to come and be painted tomorrow," said Brock. "He will know all about it. Robins have been painted on Christmas cards for many years."

After the birds' breakfast the next day Sam asked the robin to come and have a picture made.

"I will sit here on this holly branch," said the robin. "Here is the snow, and here's the holly. I can hold a sprig of mistletoe in my beak if you like."

So Sam fetched his little stool and sat in the snow with his paintbox and the badger-brush, and the robin perched on the holly branch, with a mistletoe sprig in its beak. It puffed out its scarlet breast and stared with unwinking brown eye at Sam, and he licked his brush and dipped it in the red and blue and green, giving the robin a blue feather and a green wing.

When he had finished, he thanked the robin and hid his beautiful eggshells in a hole in the wall, ready for Christmas Day.

"Have you a Christmas present for Badger?" asked Ann. "I have nearly finished my scarf, and Tom's cake is made, and Bill's hyacinth is in bud. What have you made, Sam?"

"Nothing except the Christmas card," confessed Sam. "If I could knit a pair of stockings, or grow a cabbage, or make a pasty I should know what to give him, but I can't do nothing."

"Anything," corrected Ann.

"Nothing," said Sam. "I can only play my fiddle –"

"And fall in the river and steal a few apples, and get lost and catch the wind –" laughed Ann. "Never mind. You shall share my scarf if you like, Sam, for you helped to find the

13

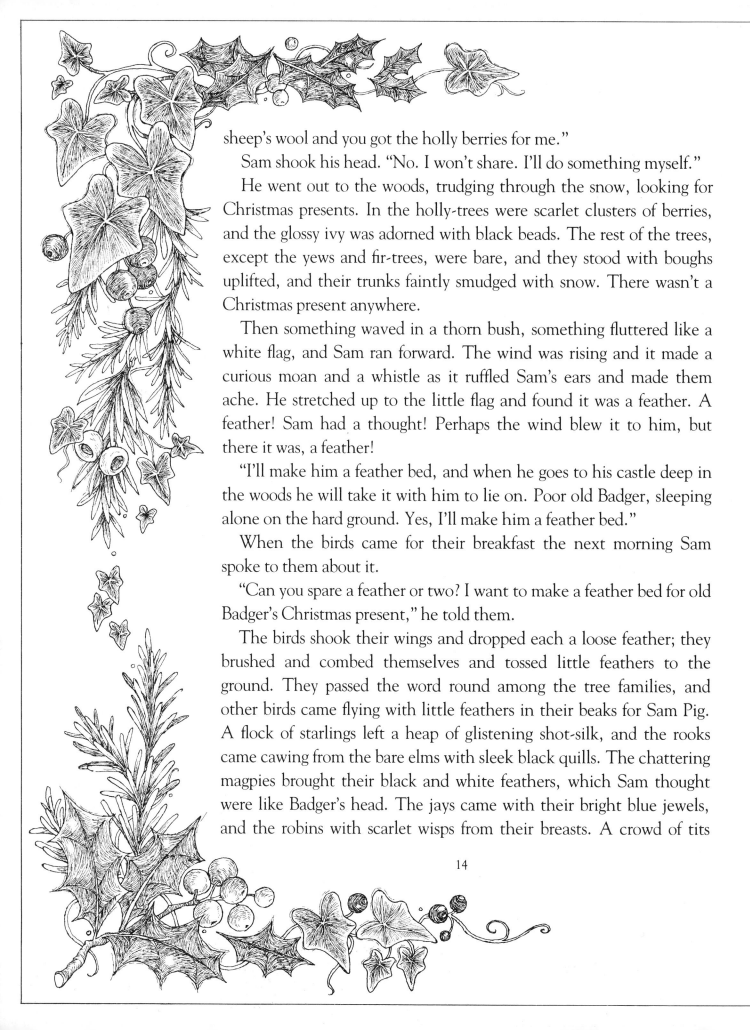

sheep's wool and you got the holly berries for me."

Sam shook his head. "No. I won't share. I'll do something myself."

He went out to the woods, trudging through the snow, looking for Christmas presents. In the holly-trees were scarlet clusters of berries, and the glossy ivy was adorned with black beads. The rest of the trees, except the yews and fir-trees, were bare, and they stood with boughs uplifted, and their trunks faintly smudged with snow. There wasn't a Christmas present anywhere.

Then something waved in a thorn bush, something fluttered like a white flag, and Sam ran forward. The wind was rising and it made a curious moan and a whistle as it ruffled Sam's ears and made them ache. He stretched up to the little flag and found it was a feather. A feather! Sam had a thought! Perhaps the wind blew it to him, but there it was, a feather!

"I'll make him a feather bed, and when he goes to his castle deep in the woods he will take it with him to lie on. Poor old Badger, sleeping alone on the hard ground. Yes, I'll make him a feather bed."

When the birds came for their breakfast the next morning Sam spoke to them about it.

"Can you spare a feather or two? I want to make a feather bed for old Badger's Christmas present," he told them.

The birds shook their wings and dropped each a loose feather; they brushed and combed themselves and tossed little feathers to the ground. They passed the word round among the tree families, and other birds came flying with little feathers in their beaks for Sam Pig. A flock of starlings left a heap of glistening shot-silk, and the rooks came cawing from the bare elms with sleek black quills. The chattering magpies brought their black and white feathers, which Sam thought were like Badger's head. The jays came with their bright blue jewels, and the robins with scarlet wisps from their breasts. A crowd of tits

14

gave him their own soft little many-coloured feathers, and even the wood pigeons left grey feathers for Sam. He had so many the air was clouded with feathers so that it seemed to be snowing again. He gathered them up and filled his sack, and even then he had some over.

On Christmas Day Sam came downstairs to the kitchen, calling "A merry Christmas" to everybody.

There stood Badger, with a twinkle in his eye. Ann gave him the black and white muffler with its little scarlet berries interwoven.

"Here's a muffler for cold days in the forest, Brock," said she.

"Just the thing for nights when I go hunting," said Brock, nodding his head and wrapping the muffler round his neck.

Then Bill gave him the little blue hyacinth growing in a pot.

"Here's a flower for you, Brock, which I've reared myself."

"Thank you, Bill. It's the flower I love," said Brock and he sniffed the sweet scent.

Then Tom came forward with the cake, which was prickly with almonds and seeds from many a plant.

"Here's a cake, Brock, and it has got so many things inside it, I've lost count of them, but there's honey-comb and eggs."

"Ah! You know how I like a slice of cake," cried Brock, taking the great round cake which was heavy as lead.

Then little Sam came with the feather bed. He had embroidered it with the letter B made of the black and white magpie feathers.

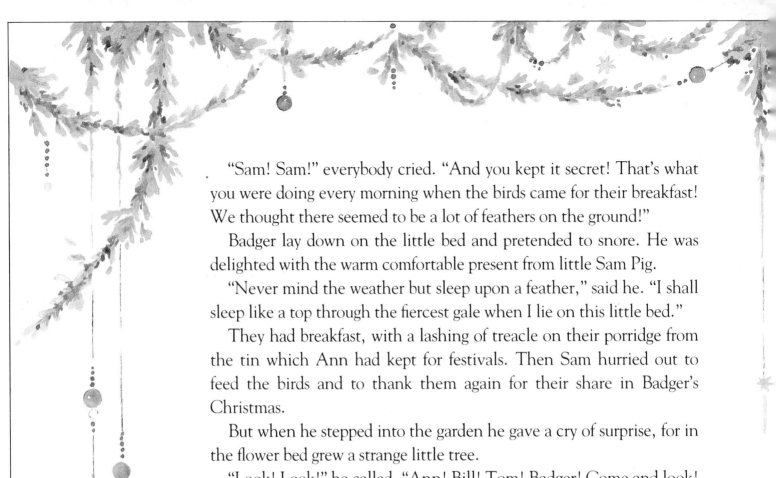

"Sam! Sam!" everybody cried. "And you kept it secret! That's what you were doing every morning when the birds came for their breakfast! We thought there seemed to be a lot of feathers on the ground!"

Badger lay down on the little bed and pretended to snore. He was delighted with the warm comfortable present from little Sam Pig.

"Never mind the weather but sleep upon a feather," said he. "I shall sleep like a top through the fiercest gale when I lie on this little bed."

They had breakfast, with a lashing of treacle on their porridge from the tin which Ann had kept for festivals. Then Sam hurried out to feed the birds and to thank them again for their share in Badger's Christmas.

But when he stepped into the garden he gave a cry of surprise, for in the flower bed grew a strange little tree.

"Look! Look!" he called. "Ann! Bill! Tom! Badger! Come and look! It wasn't growing there last night. Where has it come from? And look at the funny fruit hanging on it! What is it?"

They followed him out and stared in astonishment at the small fir-tree, all hung with pretty things. There were sugar pigs with pink noses and curly tails of string; and sugar watches with linked chains of white sugar, and chocolate mice. There were rosy apples and golden oranges,

and among the dainties were glittering icicles and frost crystals.

"Where has it come from? How did it grow here?" they asked, and they all turned to Badger. "Is it a magic?" they asked. "Will it disappear? Is it really real?"

"It's solid enough, for the tree has come from the woods," smiled Badger, "but the other things will disappear fast enough I warrant when you four get near them."

"But what about your Christmas cards, Sam?" asked Ann suddenly. "This is the time to give them."

"I sat on them, Ann," confessed Sam. "I put them on a chair and sat down on them."

"Crushed Christmas cards," murmured Tom the cook. "They will do very well to give an extra flavour to the soup. Those reds and blues and greens will make the soup taste extra good, I'm sure."

It was true. The Christmas soup with the Christmas card flavour was the nicest anyone had ever tasted, and not a drop was left.

As for the Christmas tree, everybody shared it, for the birds flew down to its branches and sang a Christmas carol in thanks for their breakfasts, and Sam sat underneath and sang another carol in thanks for their feathers.

POOR ROBIN

The north wind doth blow,
And we shall have snow,
And what will poor robin do then?
Poor thing.
He'll sit in a barn,
And keep himself warm,
And hide his head under his wing.
Poor thing.

CAROL OF THE BIRDS

From out of a wood a cuckoo did fly,
    Cuckoo,
He came to a manger with joyful cry,
    Cuckoo,
He hopped, he curtsied, round he flew,
And loud his jubilation grew,
    Cuckoo, cuckoo, cuckoo.

A pigeon flew over to Galilee,
    Vrercroo,
He strutted and cooed, and was full of glee,
    Vrercroo,
And showed with jewelled wings unfurled,
His joy that Christ was in the world,
    Vrercroo, vrercroo, vrercroo.

A dove settled down upon Nazareth,
    Tsucroo,
And tenderly chanted with all his breath,
    Tsucroo,
"Oh you," he cooed, "so good and true,
My beauty I do give to you,
    Tsucroo, tsucroo, tsucroo."

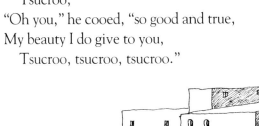

THE
LITTLE FIR
TREE

ANNA pulled her boots on hard and stumped outdoors.

"I don't want to go to school tomorrow!" she thought crossly. "I want it to be Christmas again. It's not fair . . . it went so fast, and now there's another whole year to wait!" She looked about at the damp brown garden. All dead. Her mother had said she might find the first snowdrop coming up if she looked very hard, and she did want to.

Suddenly something bright and golden caught her eye. In a corner of the garden stood the Christmas tree, where someone had thrown it on twelfth night, with its golden star still on the top.

"Oh good, I can have it for dressing up," she said, pulling the star off the prickly little tree. And then she said, "Poor tree, all bare and cold."

"Mmm . . ." sighed the tree; it was just green enough to speak still. "I'm a poor bare tree, thrown outside, and now my star's gone too, like everything else."

"Oh, don't be sad," said Anna kindly. "Think how pretty you were at Christmas, all sparkling and green."

"Yes," answered the tree wistfully, "I was very fine, wasn't I, all lit up day and night, with my coloured lights, and tiny toys, and shiny sweets

and golden decorations? The children loved me, just like the sparrows said they would."

"Which sparrows?" asked Anna, curious to hear the tree's story.

"The sparrows in the forest when I was one year old. I was green and alive and growing then, and I didn't realize how lucky I was to be at home with my family. The sparrows had been to the farmhouse nearby at Christmas time, and had peeped in at the windows. 'There's a fir tree in there,' they twittered excitedly, 'but you'd hardly recognize it. It's covered in tinsel, lights and little presents, and on the top there is a golden star. The children think it's the most beautiful tree in the whole world.' From that moment, I only wanted one thing: to be a Christmas tree. I couldn't wait to grow big enough. And I never took any notice of what the sun said to me!" whispered the tree.

21

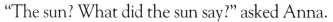

"The sun? What did the sun say?" asked Anna.

" 'Gently now, little one,' he warned in his kind smiling voice. 'You're still young; enjoy yourself while you can. Feel my warmth on your branches; feel the soft rain kissing your boughs, stretch and bend in the wind.' But all that just made me cross . . . who'd want to be stuck in a forest when they could be decorated and admired like that other fir tree?"

"I've always wanted to go to a real forest," said Anna. "Didn't you like it there?"

"No, I didn't, because I was the smallest – even when I stretched – and children used to point at me and say what a dear little tree I was, and the hare used to jump right over me, just to make it worse." The little fir tree sounded quite cross still, even though it had all happened so long ago.

"Oh, but aren't you lucky," cried Anna, trying to cheer the tree a little, "I've never seen a real hare."

"I didn't see it like that then," said the tree softly. "I couldn't wait to grow big like the others. Next year the woodman came and chose the tallest trees for ships' masts. How wonderful, I thought, they'll see the world. When shall I grow tall enough to be a mast and see the world?"

"But you never did, did you?" said Anna.

"No", whispered the forlorn tree, its voice dry and cracked, "I just waited impatiently there; waiting, waiting without seeing. The soft cold snow piled up on my branches; then the spring rain splashed down on me, and the sun warmed me. But I was just waiting for that woodman to come and choose me to be a Christmas tree, to be beautiful and admired." The fir tree sighed again, then remembered something else. "And do you know, the thrush chose me to hold her nest for her one spring, brushing through my needles, in and out, in and out, making her nest. And I sheltered her little ones . . ."

22

"You were very lucky," said Anna.

"Yes I was, but all I could think of was Christmas, Christmas, and the wonderful things the sparrows had told me about when I was little. I couldn't wait for the woodman to come back and choose me."

"And then what happened?" asked Anna, who was pressed right up close to the poor, prickly little brown tree so she could hear.

"And then," the poor tree sighed, "the woodman came at last, swinging his sharp axe. When he saw me, he said, 'There's a good one!' How proud I was, how excited, my dreams were coming true! Then he swung his axe, and felled me. How sudden it was, what cold cruel metal! I flung out my branches, but it was no use, and I crashed down hurt and dizzy." The tree was silent for a moment, and then went on more cheerfully.

"Next thing I knew I was in a warm room in a tub, and your mother was saying what a lovely tree I was. She hung me with shiny baubles that tickled my branches; and the lights, they were a bit hot, but so pretty. And then you came in with your friends, and you looked so pleased. I really bristled with pride because you all loved me so. And you danced and sang, and opened presents, and pulled the sweets off my branches: how tightly I was holding them!"

Anna put her arms round the little tree, who had once been so proud and green.

"So you did enjoy Christmas after all," she said.

"Yes, yes I did. But how soon it was over! How weak I felt afterwards, and then how homesick for my forest . . ." The tree's voice faded away.

Just then, a sharp wind blew the golden star right out of the little girl's hand, and made her shiver. And when Anna turned back to the little fir tree again, all its dry brown needles had fallen.

A VISIT FROM ST NICHOLAS

'Twas the night before Christmas, when all through
                            the house
Not a creature was stirring, not even a mouse;
The stockings were hung by the chimney with care,
In hopes that St Nicholas soon would be there;
The children were nestled all snug in their beds,
While visions of sugarplums danced in their heads;

And Mamma in her 'kerchief, and I in my cap,
Had just settled our brains for a long winter's nap;
When out on the lawn there arose such a clatter,
I sprang from the bed to see what was the matter.
Away to the window I flew like a flash,
Tore open the shutters and threw up the sash.

The moon, on the breast of the new-fallen snow,
Gave the lustre of midday to objects below,
When what to my wondering eyes should appear,
But a miniature sleigh, and eight tiny reindeer,
With a little old driver, so lively and quick,
I knew in a moment it must be St Nick.

More rapid than eagles his coursers they came,
And he whistled and shouted, and called them by name;
"Now, Dasher! Now, Dancer! Now, Prancer and Vixen!
On, Comet! On, Cupid! On, Donner and Blitzen!
To the top of the porch! To the top of the wall!
Now, dash away! Dash away! Dash away all!"

As dry leaves that before the wild hurricane fly,
When they meet with an obstacle, mount to the sky;
So up to the housetop the coursers they flew,

With the sleigh full of toys, and St Nicholas, too.
And then, in a twinkling, I heard on the roof
The prancing and pawing of each little hoof—
As I drew in my head, and was turning around,
Down the chimney St Nicholas came with a bound.

He was dressed all in fur, from his head to his foot,
And his clothes were all tarnished with ashes and soot;
A bundle of toys he had flung on his back,
And he looked like a pedlar just opening his pack.
His eyes—how they twinkled! His dimples, how merry!
His cheeks were like roses, his nose like a cherry!

His droll little mouth was drawn up like a bow,
And the beard of his chin was as white as the snow;
The stump of a pipe he held tight in his teeth,
And the smoke it encircled his head like a wreath;
He had a broad face and a little round belly
That shook, when he laughed, like a bowl full of jelly.

He was chubby and plump, a right jolly old elf,
And I laughed, when I saw him, in spite of myself;
A wink of his eye and a twist of his head,
Soon gave me to know I had nothing to dread;
He spoke not a word, but went straight to his work,
And filled all the stockings; then turned with a jerk,

And laying his finger aside of his nose,
And giving a nod, up the chimney he rose;
He sprang to his sleigh, to his team gave a whistle,
And away they all flew like the down of a thistle.
But I heard him exclaim, ere he drove out of sight,
"Happy Christmas to all, and to all a good night."

CLEMENT C. MOORE

SILENT NIGHT

Silent night, holy night,
  All is calm, all is bright
Round yon Virgin Mother and Child,
  Holy Infant, so tender and mild,
Sleep in heavenly peace,
Sleep in heavenly peace.

Silent night, holy night,
  Darkness flies, all is light.
Shepherds hear the angels sing,
  "Alleluia, hail the King!
Jesus the Saviour is born,
Jesus the Saviour is born."

Silent night, holy night,
  Wondrous star, lend thy light;
With the angels let us sing,
  Alleluia to our king.
Christ the Saviour is born,
Christ the Saviour is born.

MRS PROTHERO
AND
THE FIREMEN

IT was on the afternoon of the day of Christmas Eve, and I was in Mrs Prothero's garden, waiting for cats, with her son Jim. It was snowing. It was always snowing at Christmas. December, in my memory, is white as Lapland, though there were no reindeers. But there were cats. Patient, cold and callous, our hands wrapped in socks, we waited to snowball the cats. Sleek and long as jaguars and horrible-whiskered, spitting and snarling, they would slink and sidle over the white back-garden walls, and the lynx-eyed hunters, Jim and I, fur-capped and moccasined trappers from Hudson Bay, off Mumbles Road, would hurl our deadly snowballs at the green of their eyes.

The wise cats never appeared. We were so still, Eskimo-footed arctic marksmen in the muffling silence of the eternal snows – eternal, ever since Wednesday – that we never heard Mrs Prothero's first cry from her igloo at the bottom of the garden. Or, if we heard it at all, it was, to us, like the far-off challenge of our enemy and prey, the neighbour's polar cat. But soon the voice grew louder. "Fire!" cried Mrs Prothero, and she beat the dinner-gong.

And we ran down the garden, with the snowballs in our arms, toward the house; and smoke, indeed, was pouring out of the dining-

room, and the gong was bombilating, and Mrs Prothero was announcing ruin like a town crier in Pompeii. This was better than all the cats in Wales standing on the wall in a row. We bounded into the house, laden with snowballs, and stopped at the open door of the smoke-filled room.

Something was burning all right; perhaps it was Mr Prothero, who always slept there after midday dinner with a newspaper over his face. But he was standing in the middle of the room, saying, "A fine Christmas!" and smacking at the smoke with a slipper. "Call the fire brigade," cried Mrs Prothero as she beat the gong.

"They won't be there," said Mr Prothero, "it's Christmas."

There was no fire to be seen, only clouds of smoke and Mr Prothero standing in the middle of them, waving his slipper as though he were conducting.

"Do something," he said.

And we threw all our snowballs into the smoke – I think we missed Mr Prothero – and ran out of the house to the telephone box.

"Let's call the police as well," Jim said.

"And the ambulance."

"And Ernie Jenkins, he like fires."

But we only called the fire brigade, and soon the fire engine came and three tall men in helmets brought a hose into the house and Mr Prothero got out just in time before they turned it on. Nobody could have had a noisier Christmas Eve. And when the firemen turned off the hose and were standing in the wet, smoky room, Jim's aunt, Miss Prothero, came downstairs and peered in at them. Jim and I waited, very quietly, to hear what she would say to them. She said the right thing, always. She looked at the three tall firemen in their shining helmets, standing among the smoke and cinders and dissolving snowballs, and she said: "Would you like anything to read?"

28

KEEPING CHRISTMAS

How will you your Christmas keep?
  Feasting, fasting, or asleep?
Will you laugh or will you pray,
  Or will you forget the day?

Be it kept with joy or pray'r,
  Keep of either some to spare;
Whatsoever brings the day,
  Do not keep but give away.

ELEANOR FARJEON

30

THE HOLLY AND THE IVY

The holly and the ivy,
When they are both full grown,
Of all the trees that are in the wood,
The holly bears the crown:

*The rising of the sun
And the running of the deer,
The playing of the merry organ,
Sweet singing in the choir.*

The holly bears a blossom,
As white as the lily flower,
And Mary bore sweet Jesus Christ,
To be our sweet Saviour:

The holly bears a berry,
As red as any blood,
And Mary bore sweet Jesus Christ
To do poor sinners good:

The holly bears a prickle,
As sharp as any thorn,
And Mary bore sweet Jesus Christ
On Christmas day in the morn:

The holly bears a bark,
As bitter as any gall,
And Mary bore sweet Jesus Christ
For to redeem us all:

The holly and the ivy,
When they are both full grown,
Of all the trees that are in the wood,
The holly bears the crown.

THE NUTCRACKER

ONE hundred years ago on Christmas Eve, a little girl called Clara and her brother Fritz were having a party at their house. The room was bright with candles and the fire crackled cheerfully, as grown-ups and children joined together in all the games and dances.

Clara's eyes shone. "Isn't this lovely?" she whispered to the little wooden nutcracker hidden in her handkerchief. It was a Christmas present from her godfather.

"Look closely at the wooden head," he said as he gave it to her. "This is no ordinary nutcracker."

"His face is very sad," Clara thought, "but I like it." And from that moment she carried the little nutcracker doll with her everywhere.

"Bang, bang!" cried Fritz, who was drilling his new toy soldiers. "My soldiers are brave and handsome. Better than your ugly little doll."

"Take no notice of him," Clara said to the nutcracker. "He doesn't mean to be unkind." But the noise in the hot, crowded room made Fritz very excited. He marched up to Clara, snatched the little nutcracker and held it above his head.

"Catch it if you can!" he yelled, dancing up and down. Clara tried to grab his arm but naughty Fritz hurled the little wooden doll across

32

the room where it landed near the Christmas tree. Just then Clara's mother came up to her.

"It's supper time, Clara; come and help me," she said, and poor Clara had to leave her new toy where it had fallen.

Much later, the party was over and the children's friends went home, calling "Happy Christmas!" to each other through the snow. Clara and Fritz went to bed and it was not long before everyone in the house was asleep – everyone except Clara. She could not bear to leave the little nutcracker alone, so she crept downstairs and opened the sitting room door.

What a sight met her eyes! There were mice running everywhere, fighting and biting, and chewing all the presents under the Christmas tree! As Clara gazed in horror, she heard someone calling,

"Over here, men! Ready to charge!" It was the little nutcracker, leading the toy soldiers into battle against the mice.

"Oh good!" Clara cheered. "Don't let the mice spoil everything."

Suddenly a huge mouse wearing a golden crown leapt forward. It was the Mouse King himself, waving a sword of shining steel. The wooden swords of the toy soldiers were powerless against it and the

Nutcracker had no sword at all. In a flash, Clara tore off her slipper and threw it across the room as hard as she could. It hit the Mouse King and he dropped his sword. The Nutcracker seized it, and with one stroke he cut off the King's head. At once, the other mice stopped fighting and scurried away to their holes.

Clara turned – to find that her ugly little Nutcracker had been transformed into a handsome prince dressed in silver and white. He smiled down at her,

"You've saved my life and broken a wicked spell, little Clara. Now I am free to go back to my own country at last."

Then the prince sat Clara down under the Christmas tree and told her of his adventures.

Once upon a time, his story began, a queen quarrelled with all the mice in her palace and banished them from her kingdom. As he slunk out of the hall, a wicked old wizard mouse turned to the queen and squeaked,

"You'll be sorry for this – and so will your daughter." The queen ran to her baby's crib, but too late. The baby's tiny cheeks were thin and hairy and whiskers grew under her pointed nose. She had been turned into a rat!

The grief-stricken queen called all the wisest men in her kingdom together, and they studied their magic books till they came upon a way to break the wizard mouse's spell. A Krakatuk tree must be found, and one of its nuts must be picked. Then someone strong enough must crack open the nut and give the kernel to the rat princess. As soon as she ate it, the spell would be broken. The wise men searched. All the queen's subjects searched. At long last they found a Krakatuk tree nut and a young prince to open it. Crack, crack. He split the shell and

gave the Krakatuk nut to the rat princess. She ate it, and instantly became a little baby again.

"Oh thank you, thank you," cried the queen. But as she spoke the prince grew smaller and smaller, until he had turned into a little wooden nutcracker. They heard the wizard mouse squeaking with laughter,

"You may have your princess back, but you've lost the prince, and one day King Mouse will cut off his head!"

"So I became an ugly little nutcracker," the prince went on. "One day your godfather found me. He was sure you wouldn't mind my ugly face, Clara, and he was right. Thank you for saving my life. . . I must return to my own country now, so would you like to come with me to the Kingdom of Sweets and visit my Sugar Palace?"

Clara was too excited to speak, but she nodded, her eyes shining. At once the Christmas tree grew taller and taller and its lights glittered like bright stars. The walls of the sitting room disappeared. Clara and the prince were floating in the shimmering moonlight in a walnut-shell boat. Around them, snowflake fairies danced to sweet music and gently guided the boat to the shore of Candyland. The prince and Clara stepped out and walked up an avenue of trees laden with toffee apples, glittering sugar plums and chocolate nuts. They passed cottages whose walls were chocolate bars, with barley-sugar windows. The breezes smelt of honey and strawberry jam.

"It's . . . it's delicious," Clara whispered, her eyes darting here, there and everywhere. The nutcracker prince laughed,

"Wait until you see my palace!" And he pointed through the trees to a mass of glittering towers. A beautiful Sugar Plum Fairy came towards them and smiled at Clara.

"My snowflake fairies have told me what you did, and I want to thank you for saving our prince." She led the little girl to a magnificent throne inside the palace. "Tonight you are Queen Clara!"

Then the celebrations began. Sugar sticks twirled, chocolate drop cymbals clashed. A Chinese teapot and a set of Arabian coffee cups waltzed together, a troupe of Cossacks leapt across the floor. Spun-sugar roses curtsied gracefully as the prince invited the Sugar Plum Fairy to dance. How all the people clapped and cheered!

"Welcome to our prince," they cried. "Hurrah for the Nutcracker! Hurrah for Clara! Hurrah! Hurrah!"

Clara blinked; her eyes were dazzled.

"Hurrah! It's Christmas Day," she heard her brother Fritz shouting as she opened her eyes. The dancers, the Sugar Plum Fairy and the prince were all gone, and not a trace of the Sugar Palace remained.

"It must have been a dream," thought Clara sadly.

Time passed, and Clara quite forgot the little nutcracker.

But many years later, on her wedding day, she smiled a secret smile because the sugary towers of the wedding cake reminded her of the prince's palace and, on the top, she was sure she glimpsed a tiny sugar plum fairy dancing.

36

CHRISTMAS IS COMING

Christmas is coming,
The geese are getting fat,
Please to put a penny
In the old man's hat.
If you haven't got a penny,
A ha'penny will do;
If you haven't got a ha'penny,
Then God bless you!

IN THE BLEAK MIDWINTER

In the bleak midwinter
   Frosty wind made moan,
Earth stood hard as iron,
   Water like a stone;
Snow had fallen, snow on snow,
   Snow on snow,
In the bleak midwinter
   Long ago.

Our God, heaven cannot hold Him,
   Nor earth sustain;
Heaven and earth shall flee away
   When He comes to reign:
In the bleak mid winter
   A stable-place sufficed
The Lord God Almighty
   Jesus Christ.

What can I give Him,
   Poor as I am?
If I were a shepherd
   I would bring a lamb;
If I were a wise man
   I would do my part—
Yet what I can, I give Him,
   Give my heart.

CHRISTINA ROSSETTI

BRER RABBIT'S CHRISTMAS

ONCE upon a bright clear winter morning Brer Fox stole into Brer Rabbit's garden and dug up a big sackful of his best carrots. Brer Rabbit didn't see him as he was visiting his friend Brer Bear at the time. When he got home he was mighty angry to see his empty carrot-patch.

"Brer Fox! That's who's been here," cried Brer Rabbit, and his whiskers twitched furiously. "Here are his paw marks and some hairs from his tail. All my best winter carrots gone! I'll make him give them back or my name's not Brer Rabbit."

He went along, lippity lip, clippity clip, and as he went along his little nose wrinkled at the fragrant smell of soup coming from Brer Fox's house.

"Now see here," he called crossly. "I just know it's my carrots you're cooking. I want them back so you'd better open your door."

"Too bad," chuckled Brer Fox. "I'm not opening my door until winter is over. I have plenty of carrots thanks to my kind friend Brer Rabbit, and a stack of other food for Christmas as well. I'm keeping my windows shut and my door bolted, so do go away. I want to enjoy my first bowl of carrot soup in peace."

At this, Brer Rabbit kicked the door, blim blam. He hammered on the door, bangety bang. It wasn't any use. My, he was in a rage as he turned away. Kind friend Brer Rabbit indeed! He stomped off, muttering furiously. But soon he grew thoughtful, then he gave a hop or two followed by a little dance. By the time he reached home he was in a mighty good temper. Brer Rabbit had a plan all worked out. He'd get his carrots back and annoy Brer Fox into the bargain!

On Christmas Eve, Brer Rabbit heaved a sack of stones on his shoulder and climbed up onto Brer Fox's roof. He clattered round the chimney making plenty of noise.

"Who's there?" Brer Fox called. "Go away at once. I'm cooking my supper."

"It's Father Christmas," replied Brer Rabbit in a gruff voice. "I've brought a sack full of presents for Brer Fox."

"Oh, that's different," said Brer Fox quickly. "You're most welcome. Come right along down the chimney."

"I can't. I'm stuck," Brer Rabbit said in his gruff Father Christmas voice. Brer Fox unbolted his door and went outside to take a look. Certainly he could see somebody on the roof so he rushed back inside and called,

"Well, Father Christmas, don't trouble to come down the chimney yourself. Just drop the sack of presents and I'll surely catch it."

"Can't. That's stuck too," yelled Brer Rabbit and he smiled to himself. "You'll have to climb up inside your chimney, Brer Fox, then catch hold of the piece of string around the sack and you can haul it down yourself."

"That's easy," Brer Fox cried, "here I come," and he disappeared up the chimney.

Like lightning, Brer Rabbit was off that roof and in through the open doorway. There were his carrots in a sack, and on the table was a

40

fine cooked goose and a huge Christmas pudding. He grabbed them both, stuffed them into the sack and he ran. Chickle, chuckle, how he did run.

That old Brer Fox struggled up the chimney, higher and higher. He couldn't see any string but he felt it hanging down so he gave a big tug. The sack opened and out tumbled all the stones, clatter bang, bim bam, right on Brer Fox's head. My, my, he certainly went down that chimney quickly. Poor Brer Fox! He'd lost his Christmas dinner and the carrots, and now he had a sore head.

That rascally Brer Rabbit laughed and laughed but he made sure he kept out of Brer Fox's way all that Christmas Day and for some time afterwards.

CHRISTMAS DAY

Last night in the open shippen
  The Infant Jesus lay,
While cows stood at the hay-crib
  Twitching the sweet hay.

As I trudged through the snow-fields
  That lay in their own light,
A thorn-bush with its shadow
  Stood doubled on the night.

And I stayed on my journey
  To listen to the cheep
Of a small bird in the thorn-bush
  I woke from its puffed sleep.

The bright stars were my angels
  And with the heavenly host
I sang praise to the Father,
  The Son and Holy Ghost.

ANDREW YOUNG

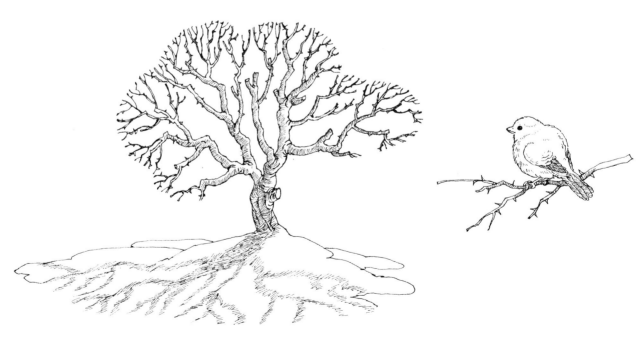

CAROL OF THE FIELD MICE

from *The Wind in the Willows*

Villagers all, this frosty tide,
Let your doors swing open wide,
Though wind may follow, and snow beside,
Yet draw us in by your fire to bide;
    Joy shall be yours in the morning!

Here we stand in the cold and the sleet,
Blowing fingers and stamping feet,
Come from far away you to greet –
You by the fire and we in the street –
    Bidding you joy in the morning!

For ere one half of the night was gone,
Sudden a star has led us on,
Raining bliss and benison –
Bliss tomorrow and more anon,
    Joy for every morning!

Goodman Joseph toiled through the snow –
Saw the star o'er a stable low;
Mary she might not further go –
Welcome thatch, and litter below!
    Joy was hers in the morning!

And then they heard the angels tell
"Who were the first to cry Nowell?
Animals all, as it befell,
In the stable where they did dwell!
    Joy shall be theirs in the morning!"

KENNETH GRAHAME

A Very Big Cat

MANY years ago a hunter from the Northlands trapped a great white bear. It was such a fine bear that he decided to present it to the king of his country. So the man and the bear set out even though it was winter and the snow was falling thick and fast. They tramped and tramped but the king's palace was far away and it began to grow dark. The hunter was cold and weary. Suddenly through the trees he glimpsed a little cottage with lights a-shining.

"I'll ask for shelter for the night," he told the big white bear as he knocked on the door. It was opened by a tall thin man with a very worried face.

"Please may we come in? We are both very tired with trudging through the snow," said the hunter.

"Oh no, no," replied the man whose name was Halvor.

"We are going to see the king, this fine bear and I. We only want to warm ourselves at your fire for the night."

"Impossible! You can't stay here." Halvor waved his arms about, "I can't help you." The bear gave a sad little grunt, while the hunter shivered and stared at Halvor in surprise. He tried again.

44

"We don't need much room and we won't disturb you. Please don't turn us away into the snow." Halvor shook his head.

"I'm not an unkind man. I'd like to help you, but it's Christmas Eve, a time of great trouble for me." He opened the door wider. "Look at my wife and my three children hurrying to get things ready for Christmas. See how sad and worried they look," Halvor went on. "They never enjoy Christmas because year after year the trolls come. Many, many trolls. They chase us out, throw our food about, then break all the dishes. They tear down the decorations, they scream, they shout. Oh no, Christmas is not a happy time for us."

"Trolls!" exclaimed the hunter. "Trolls don't frighten us. Please let us into your warm house. Trolls won't bother us, will they, Bear?"

At last Halvor let them both in and they slept in a warm corner near the stove. Halvor's wife had prepared a delicious dinner and on Christmas Day she put everything on the table, which the children decorated with holly and candles. All of a sudden, quicker than a flash, the trolls appeared. They came down the chimney, in at the windows, under the door and even up through the floorboards. Some were tall and some were small. Some had long noses and no tails; some had long tails and long ears. All of them were very, very ugly. Halvor and his family grabbed their warmest clothes and ran and locked themselves in the woodshed.

Then those trolls attacked. They bellowed. They screamed. They threw the turkey and vegetables about and smashed the dishes. They squashed jellies into the floor and blew bubbles in the milk. They jumped on the table and paddled in the custard. Some smaller trolls emptied jars of jam and rubbed it over the windows. The noise was terrible but the man and his bear watched quietly by the stove. At last, when there was nothing left to damage, the naughtiest troll of all saw the big bear lying peacefully in the corner. He grabbed a sausage, pushed it on a fork and waved it right under the bear's nose.

"Pussy, pussy, have a sausage," he shouted in a silly voice. The bear sniffed. It was a good smell. At once the troll pulled the sausage away, out of the bear's reach.

"Pussy, pussy, here you are." Again the troll waved the sausage in front of the bear and again he snatched it away. Slowly the bear lumbered to his feet. He opened his mouth wider and wider. He let out a great roar, then another even louder one. He chased those trolls up the chimney, out of the windows and under the floorboards, from the smallest to the largest, until there was not one left.

"You are a fine bear," the hunter said proudly. "Here, have a sausage or two." So the bear ate sausages; then he licked some jam from the windows because bears love sweet things.

"You can come out of the woodshed now," the hunter shouted. "My bear has chased away all the trolls."

Halvor, his wife and three children crept back to the cottage. They could hardly believe the trolls had gone, but when they saw it was true they set about cleaning up the mess with a will. There was enough food for a good supper before they all went to bed, and the next day the hunter and the bear went on their way to the king. Halvor never saw them again.

A year later, on Christmas Eve, Halvor was chopping wood in the forest when he heard someone calling his name. "Halvor! Halvor!"

"Yes, I'm Halvor. What do you want?" he replied.

"Is that big white cat still living with you?" It was a troll's voice.

"She certainly is," shouted Halvor. "And she has seven kittens now, each one bigger and fiercer than the last. Do you want to visit her?"

"No! We'll never come to your house again," the trolls screamed. And they never did. Ever afterwards Halvor, his wife and their three children enjoyed their Christmas Day in peace and contentment.

DON'T TELL

Christmas eve
Christmas day
don't tell mum I'm running away.

I'm afraid of Father Christmas
coming down the chimney
while I'm fast asleep
he might come and grab me.

Christmas eve
Christmas day
don't tell mum
I'm running away.

MICHAEL ROSEN

GOOD KING WENCESLAS

Good King Wenceslas looked out
    On the Feast of Stephen,
When the snow lay round about,
    Deep and crisp and even;
Brightly shone the moon that night,
    Though the frost was cruel,
When a poor man came in sight,
    Gathering winter fuel.

"Hither, page, and stand by me,
    If thou know'st it, telling,
Yonder peasant, who is he?
    Where and what his dwelling?"

"Sire, he lives a good league hence,
    Underneath the mountain,
Right against the forest fence,
    By Saint Agnes' fountain."

"Bring me flesh and bring me wine,
    Bring me pine logs hither;
Thou and I will see him dine,
    When we bear them thither."
Page and monarch forth they went,
    Forth they went together,
Through the rude wind's wild lament
    And the bitter weather.

"Sire, the night is darker now,
    And the wind blows stronger;
Fails my heart, I know not how,
    I can go no longer."
"Mark my footsteps, good my page!
    Tread thou in them boldly:
Thou shalt find the winter's rage
    Freeze thy blood less coldly."

In his master's steps he trod,
    Where the snow lay dinted;
Heat was in the very sod
    Which the saint had printed.
Therefore, Christian men, be sure,
    Wealth or rank possessing,
Ye who now will bless the poor,
    Shall yourselves find blessing.

THE FAIRY SHIP

LITTLE Tom was the son of a sailor. He lived in a small white-washed cottage in Cornwall, on the rocky cliffs looking over the sea. From his bedroom window he could watch the great waves with their curling plumes of white foam, and count the seagulls as they circled in the blue sky. Tom's father was somewhere out on that great stretch of ocean, and all Tom's thoughts were there, following him, wishing for him to come home. Every day he ran down the narrow path to the small rocky bay, and sat there waiting for the ship to return.

December brought wild winds that swept the coast. Little Tom was kept indoors, for the gales would have blown him away like a gull's feather if he had gone to the rocky pathway. He was deeply disappointed that he couldn't keep watch in his favourite place. A letter had come, saying that his father was on his way home and any time he might arrive. Tom feared he wouldn't be there to see him, and he stood by the window for hours watching the sky and the wild tossing sea.

"What shall I have for Christmas, Mother?" he asked one day. "Will Father Christmas remember to bring me something?"

"Perhaps he will, if our ship comes home in time," smiled his mother, and then she sighed and looked out at the wintry scene.

"Will he come in a sleigh with eight reindeer pulling it?" persisted Tom.

"Maybe he will," said his mother, but she wasn't thinking what she was saying. Tom knew at once, and he pulled her skirt.

"Father Christmas won't come in a sleigh, because there isn't any snow here. Besides, it is too rocky, and the reindeer would slip. I think he'll come in a ship, a grand ship with blue sails and a gold mast."

Tom's mother suddenly laughed aloud.

"Of course he will, little Tom. Father Christmas comes in a sleigh drawn by a team of reindeer to the children of towns and villages, but to the children of the sea he sails in a ship with all the presents tucked away in the hold."

She took her little son up in her arms and kissed him, but he struggled away and went back to the window.

Christmas morning came, and it was a day of surprising sunshine and calm. The seas danced into the cove in sparkling waves, and fluttered their flags of white foam, and tossed their treasures of seaweed and shells on the narrow beach.

Tom's mother's face was happy and excited, as if she had a secret. Her eyes shone with joy, and she seemed to dance round the room in excitement, but she said nothing.

Tom ate his breakfast quietly – a bantam egg and some honey for a special treat. Then he ran outside, to the gate, and down the slippery grassy path which led to the sea.

"Where are you going, Tom?" called his mother. "You wait here, and you'll see something."

"No, Mother. I'm going to look for the ship, the little Christmas ship," he answered, and away he trotted.

The water was deep blue, like the sky, and purple shadows hovered over it, as the waves gently rocked the cormorants fishing there. The little boy leaned back in his sheltered spot, and the sound of the water made him drowsy. The sweet air lulled him and his head began to droop.

Then he saw a sight so beautiful he had to rub his eyes to get the sleep out of them. The wintry sun made a pathway on the water, flickering with points of light on the crests of the waves, and down this golden lane came a tiny ship that seemed no larger than a toy. She moved swiftly through the water, making for the cove, and Tom cried out with joy and clapped his hands as she approached.

The wind filled the blue satin sails, and the sunbeams caught the mast of gold. On deck was a company of sailors dressed in white, and

they were making music of some kind, for shrill squeaks and whistles and pipings came through the air. Tom leaned forward to watch them, and as the ship came nearer he could see that the little sailors were playing flutes, tootling a hornpipe, then whistling a carol.

He stared very hard at their pointed faces, and little pink ears. They were not sailor-men at all, but a crew of white mice! There were four-and-twenty of them – yes, twenty-four white mice with gold rings round their snowy necks, and gold rings in their ears!

The little ship sailed into the cove, through the barriers of sharp rocks, and the white mice hurried backward and forward, hauling at the silken ropes, casting the gold anchor, crying with high voices as the ship came to port close to the rock where Tom sat waiting and watching.

Out came the Captain – and would you believe it? He was a Duck, with a cocked hat and a blue jacket trimmed with gold braid. Tom

knew at once he was Captain Duck because under his wing he carried a brass telescope, and by his side was a tiny sword.

"Quack! Quack!" said the Captain, saluting Tom, and Tom of course stood up and saluted back.

"The ship's cargo is ready, Sir," said the Duck. "We have sailed across the sea to wish you a merry Christmas. Quick! Quick!" he said, turning to the ship, and the four-and-twenty white mice scurried down to the cabin and dived into the hold.

Then up on deck they came, staggering under their burdens, dragging small bales of provisions, little oaken casks, baskets, sacks and hampers. They brought their packages ashore and laid them on the smooth sand near Tom's feet.

There were almonds and raisins, bursting from silken sacks. There were sugar-plums and goodies, pouring out of wicker baskets. There was a host of tiny toys, drums and marbles, tops and balls, pearly shells, and a flying kite, a singing bird and a musical-box.

When the last toy had been safely carried from the ship the white mice scampered back. They weighed anchor, singing "Yo-heave-ho!" and they ran up the rigging. The Captain cried "Quack! Quack!" and he stood on the ship's bridge. Before Tom could say "Thank you," the little golden ship began to sail away, with flags flying, and the blue satin sails tugging at the silken cords. The four-and-twenty white mice waved their sailor hats to Tom, and the Captain looked at him through his spy-glass.

Away went the ship, swift as the wind, a glittering speck on the waves. Tom waited till he could see her no more, and then he stooped over his presents. He tasted the almonds and raisins, he sucked the goodies, he beat the drum, and tinkled the musical-box and the iron triangle. He was so busy playing that he did not hear soft footsteps behind him.

Suddenly he was lifted up in a pair of strong arms and pressed against a thick blue coat, and two bright eyes were smiling at him.

"Well, Thomas, my son! Here I am! You didn't expect me, now did you? A Happy Christmas, Tom, boy. I crept down soft as a snail, and you never heard a tinkle of me, did you?"

"Oh, Father!" Tom flung his arms round his father's neck and kissed him many times. "Oh, Father. I knew you were coming. Look! They've been, they came just before you, in the ship."

"Who, Tom? Who's been? I caught you fast asleep. Come along home and see what Father Christmas has brought you. He came along o' me, in my ship, you know. He gave me some presents for you."

"He's been here already, just now, in a little gold ship, Father," cried Tom, stammering with excitement. "He's just sailed away. He was a Duck, Captain Duck, and there were four-and-twenty white mice with him. He left me all these toys. Lots of toys and things."

Tom struggled to the ground, and pointed to the sand, but where the treasure of the fairy ship had been stored there was only a heap of pretty shells and seaweed and striped pebbles.

56

"They's all gone," he cried, choking back a sob, but his father laughed and carried him off, pick-a-back, up the narrow footpath.

On the table in the kitchen lay such a medley of presents that Tom opened his eyes wider than ever. There were almonds and raisins, and goodies in little coloured sacks, and a musical-box with a picture of a ship on its round lid. There was a drum with scarlet edges, and a book, and a pearly shell from a far island, and a kite of thin paper from China, and a love-bird in a cage. Best of all there was a little model of his father's ship, which his father had carved for Tom.

"Why, these are like the toys from the fairy ship," cried Tom. "Those were little ones, like fairy toys, and these are big, real ones."

"Then it must have been a dream-ship," said his mother. "You must tell us all about it."

So little Tom told the tale of the ship with blue satin sails and gold mast, and he told of the four-and-twenty white mice with gold rings round their necks, and the Captain Duck, who said "Quack! Quack!"

When Tom had finished, his father said, "I'll sing you a song of that fairy-ship, our Tom. Then you'll never forget what you saw."

There was a ship a-sailing,
A-sailing on the sea.
And it was deeply laden,
With pretty things for me.

There were raisins in the cabin,
And almonds in the hold,
The sails were made of satin,
And the mast it was of gold.

The four-and-twenty sailors
That stood between the decks
Were four-and-twenty white mice
With rings about their necks.

The Captain was a Duck, a Duck,
With a jacket on his back,
And when this fairy-ship set sail,
The Captain he said "Quack".

It was such a lovely song that Tom hummed it all that happy
Christmas Day, and it just fitted into the tune on his musical-box. He
sang it to his children when they were little, long years later, and you
can sing it too if you like!

I Saw Three Ships

I saw three ships come sailing in
    On Christmas day, on Christmas day;
I saw three ships come sailing in
    On Christmas day in the morning.

And what was in those ships all three
    On Christmas day, on Christmas day;
And what was in those ships all three
    On Christmas day in the morning?

Our Saviour Christ and his ladie,
    On Christmas day, on Christmas day;
Our Saviour Christ and his ladie,
    On Christmas day in the morning.

And all the bells on earth shall ring
    On Christmas day, on Christmas day;
And all the bells on earth shall ring
    On Christmas day in the morning.

A Cradle Song

Sweet dreams, form a shade
O'er my lovely infant's head;
Sweet dreams of pleasant streams
By happy, silent, moony beams.

Sweet sleep, with soft down
Weave thy brows an infant crown.
Sweet sleep, Angel mild,
Hover o'er my happy child.

Sweet smiles, in the night
Hover over my delight;
Sweet smiles, mother's smiles,
All the livelong night beguiles.

Sweet moans, dovelike sighs,
Chase not slumber from thy eyes.
Sweet moans, sweeter smiles,
All the dovelike moans beguiles.

Sweet babe, in thy face
Holy image I can trace.
Sweet babe once like thee,
Thy Maker lay and wept for me,

Wept for me, for thee, for all,
When He was an infant small.
Thou His image ever see,
Heavenly face that smiles on thee,

Smiles on thee, on me, on all;
Who became an infant small.
Infant smiles are His own smiles;
Heaven and earth to peace beguiles.

WILLIAM BLAKE

59

EARLY ON CHRISTMAS MORNING

Two days before Christmas Mrs Venn sat by the fire and wrapped up family presents. Tacker worked at a model Tiger Moth on a sheet of newspaper spread out on the brown chenille tablecloth.

"There, there's Granfer's," Mrs Venn said with satisfaction, adding a small parcel of tobacco and hand-knitted socks to the pile beside her. "I want for you to go over and give him that, Tacker, early Christmas morning."

"Me?" Tacker looked round in alarm. "You coming too?"

"No need for me to come, is there?"

"You always have."

"Well, yes, but I reckon you're old enough now to take your grandfather his presents without me being there."

"I won't know what to say."

"What to say? Bless me, boy, say 'Merry Christmas'. You don't need for to make a speech. You're not scared of Granfer all of a sudden, are you?"

And so, two mornings later, in the cockcrow dark, with only a slice of bread and butter and a cup of tea inside him, Tacker set off for his grandfather's cottage. It was a morning of black frost under a cloudy

sky, and daylight came slowly. From most cottage windows he passed, lamplight or candle-light shone out, some upstairs, some down. He was surprised when he reached his grandfather's cottage to see that *his* light was still upstairs, since his grandfather was usually up early.

Tacker called "Granfer?"

"Tacker? Come up then. I'm still in bed."

The boy groped his way up the short, steep flight of stairs, opened the door of his grandfather's room and advanced uncertainly to the bedside. "Merry Christmas this is for you," he said in one breath, and put the package on the counterpane.

"Merry Christmas," the old man said. He was smoking his first pipe of the day. He took it out of his mouth and propped it in the tray of the flowery china candlestick beside him while he picked up the package and turned it over in his hands.

"What's this, eh? Present? Your Mam send you? That's it, then. Now, seeing I'm a bit slow this morning, will you do something for me?" He handed Tacker a box of matches. "Go down and put a light to the oil stove, and set the kettle on for me tea, will you?"

Tacker went carefully down the stairs and along to the tiny kitchen.

61

Outside the closed door he stopped in surprise. Under the latch was a small hole, and yellow light showed through. Who had lighted the kitchen lamp, if his grandfather had not been down? It could not have burned all night – it would have run out of oil. He listened. No sound. Was someone there? He was fearful and yet curious, and he longed to run upstairs again. But that would look daft.

Cautiously he raised the latch and peered into the room. The lamp burned on the table; there was no one there, but propped against the table stood a bicycle. Completely bewildered, he gazed at it. A *bicycle*, in Granfer's kitchen? He didn't ride a bicycle. Or at least he hadn't for a long time – not since the night he tumbled off into the stream before the wall was built alongside the village street. Tacker could remember hearing about that; he had been about four at the time. But what had happened to Granfer's bike after that he did not know.

This one was not new, but it gleamed with a fresh coat of yellow enamel, picked out with white. The handlebars and wheel rims shone bright; the tyres looked unused. There was no pump or lamp. Pinned to the saddle was a piece of paper.

He went forward and read the message on it.

"For Tacker. Happy Christmas from Granfer."

A bicycle. *Now.* He did not need to wait until his birthday, after all.

He crouched down, examining it. It had been beautifully cared for, oiled and greased and kept free from rust, even before it was repainted. But his grandfather always took care of things; he liked to tell of the way he had cared for his fine stallions when he walked them as a younger man. The churchyard, tended by him, was well weeded and full of flowers, and he scythed the grass close, even on such forgotten graves as John Hobson's.

Tacker stood up and took hold of the hand-grips, and bounced the front wheel on its deep-patterned tyres. His, his, his. He could ride out, down the street, all round the village like the others did (and as he had done before now, but only on borrowed bikes); round and round, swooping and whooping. He turned, ready to wheel it out, but remembered. He hadn't even said thank you.

The door opened and his grandfather came in. He had put on trousers and the fisherman's jersey he wore for gardening.

"Well, will it do?" he asked.

Tacker did a thing he had not done for a long time. He flung his arms round his grandfather and hugged him. He said "Thank 'ee, Granfer, thank 'ee," over and over again.

"I'm sorry I couldn't manage to put on a pump, and a lamp," said his grandfather.

"That don't matter," Tacker said, thinking that the lamp, at least, mattered a good deal; as he couldn't ride after dark without it, that meant that at this time of year he wouldn't be able to go out after four o'clock.

"You've done it up handsome," he said. "Is it the bike that – is it the one you used to ride?"

The old man nodded. "That's the one. It was a wet night, and dark and slippy, and I came off in the stream. Didn't hurt the bike much, but it shook me bones. Wet to the skin, I was, and cold, so I got rheumatiz. Just didn't ever want to ride it again, after that."

He saw Tacker to the gate. "You can ride that thing, I suppose?"

Tacker swung a leg over the saddle to show him.

"Um. Beats me how you all learn it. Well, straight home, mind. Don't go gallivanting off."

Tacker only smiled by way of answer, and waved as he let the cycle carry him away downhill until he was out of sight. Go straight home on his first ride on his own bicycle? Of course not. He must have one circuit of the village, at least.

He stood up out of the saddle and rushed full tilt down the hill below the forge; then pedalled hard up the opposite slope, and just reached the top without dismounting. Sharp right along the north ridge, past cob walls, stone walls, hedges, and then round the corner by the dipping place and so home.

Elated, hungry, and breathless, he ran into the indoor warmth.

His mother came out of the kitchen and smiled broadly at sight of him.

"You managed that errand for me, did you?" she asked.

He hugged her, too. "It's lovely, the bike. I never guessed. Have you seen it, all done up? Come and look."

"Ah that'll do later. Breakfast's keeping warm on the range. Come in and we'll have our presents before anything else."

When it was Tacker's turn to be given his parcels, he opened the two from his parents first. In one was a bicycle pump; in the other, a lamp.

64

A CHRISTMAS CAROL

The Christ-child lay on Mary's lap,
  His hair was like a light.
(O weary, weary were the world,
  But here is all aright.)

The Christ-child lay on Mary's breast,
  His hair was like a star.
(O stern and cunning are the kings,
  But here the true hearts are.)

The Christ-child lay on Mary's heart,
  His hair was like a fire.
(O weary, weary is the world,
  But here the world's desire.)

The Christ-child stood at Mary's knee,
  His hair was like a crown,
And all the flowers looked up at him,
  And all the stars looked down.

G. K. CHESTERTON

I Sing of a Maiden

I sing of a maiden
That is makeless;
King of all kings
To her son she chose.

He came all so still
Where his mother was,
As dew in April
That falleth on the grass.

He came all so still
To his mother's bower,
As dew in April
That falleth on the flower.

He came all so still
Where his mother lay,
As dew in April
That falleth on the spray.

Mother and maiden
Was never none but she;
Well may such a lady
God's mother be.

makeless: matchless

THE ELVES AND THE SHOEMAKER

ONCE upon a time there was a shoemaker who worked hard and made very good shoes. All day he toiled in his shop, but times were bad and he grew poorer and poorer. At last, the evening came when he cut out a pair of shoes from his last bit of leather. He put the pieces on his bench to sew in the morning when the light was better, and laid everything out ready, including the needles and thread.

"I may never make another pair of shoes," he sighed as he put the shutters over the shop window. "When I sell these, I must use all the money to buy food for my family, and there will be nothing left over for more leather. Oh dear, what shall I do?"

The next morning he woke with a heavy heart and went sadly to his bench. To his amazement, instead of the pile of leather pieces, he found the most beautiful pair of shoes, exquisitely sewn with the tiniest, neatest stitches he had ever seen. The shoemaker was quite bewildered, but he took down his shutters and put the shoes in the shop window.

He was still puzzling over who could have made them when the door opened and in came a rich old gentleman. He wanted to buy the shoes, and offered the shoemaker four times as much as he had ever been paid for a pair of shoes in his life. The shoemaker was overjoyed. He rushed straight out and bought more leather and enough food to feed his family for several days.

That evening he sat at his bench and cut out two pairs of shoes from the new leather. He left the pieces laid out as before, ready to sew the next day.

In the morning he was even more amazed to find two beautiful pairs of shoes sitting on the bench.

"Whoever can it be," he wondered, "who works so fast and sews such tiny stitches?"

Again he put the shoes in the shop window, and rich people who had never visited his shop before came in and paid a lot of money for them. The shoemaker went off again and bought more leather and cut out more shoes. Every night for weeks the same thing happened. Two pairs, sometimes four pairs, were made in a night, and the shoemaker was soon well known all over the town for his excellent shoes.

But he still had no idea who was making the shoes, and he grew more curious day by day. One evening he could bear it no longer, and he and his wife stayed awake and peeped behind the door to see who their helpful night visitors were. As the clock struck midnight, they heard a scuffling and a scurrying from the window, and saw two little men squeezing through the shutters. They hurried over to the bench, took a set of tiny tools from their workbag and began stitching and hammering. The shoemaker and his wife rubbed their eyes to make sure they weren't dreaming, for the little men were no bigger than the shoemaker's needles! The elves – for that is what they were – worked hard till just before dawn when three beautiful pairs of shoes stood ready on the bench. Then they packed their tools away, tidied up the mess, and vanished the way they had come.

When they had recovered from their amazement, the shoemaker and his wife wondered how they could show their gratitude to the elves. As it was just before Christmas, the shoemaker's wife suggested that they should make some tiny clothes as presents for the raggedy

little fellows. So all the next day she busied herself making two little green jackets and two pairs of trousers, while the shoemaker stitched two tiny pairs of boots.

On Christmas Eve, they laid the presents out on the shoemaker's bench together with two tiny glasses of wine and a plate of little cakes and biscuits. That night, they kept watch again. The elves scrambled into the shop and climbed onto the bench as they had done before. When they saw the little green jackets and trousers and the tiny boots, they shouted and danced for joy. They put the clothes on; they drank the wine and ate the food; then they disappeared in a flash.

After Christmas, the shoemaker still cut out shoes and left the pieces on his bench, but the elves never came back. They knew the shoemaker and his wife had seen them because the clothes were exactly the right size – and elves do not like to be seen by humans.

The shoemaker did not really mind, for his shop was now so well-known that he had plenty of customers. His stitches were not as neat as the elves' stitches, but no one seemed to notice. He and his family were never poor again and every year after that on Christmas Eve, they would gather round the fire and drink a toast to the little elves who had helped them when times were hard.

CHRISTMAS MORN

Shall I tell you what will come
to Bethlehem on Christmas morn,
who will kneel them gently down
before the Lord new-born?

One small fish from the river,
with scales of red, red gold,
one wild bee from the heather,
one grey lamb from the fold,
one ox from the high pasture,
one black bull from the herd,
one goatling from the far hills,
one white, white bird.

And many children – God give them grace,
bringing tall candles to light Mary's face.

RUTH SAWYER

AWAY IN A MANGER

Away in a manger,
No crib for a bed,
The little Lord Jesus
Laid down his sweet head.
The stars in the bright sky
Look'd down where he lay,
The little Lord Jesus
Asleep on the hay.

The cattle are lowing,
The baby awakes,
But little Lord Jesus
No crying he makes.
I love thee, Lord Jesus,
Look down from the sky,
And stay by my cradle
Till morning is nigh.

Be near me, Lord Jesus,
I ask thee to stay
Close by me for ever,
And love me, I pray.
Bless all the dear children
In thy tender care,
And fit us for heaven,
To live with thee there.

THE STONES OF PLOUHINEC

In parts of Brittany are found groups of the great stones known as menhirs, arranged in circles or avenues, like tall, rough-hewn pillars. Country people will tell you that long ago they were set up by the kerions, the fairy dwarfs, and that beneath them the kerions hid their gold and treasure. Each group of stones has its own legend, and this is the story of the Stones of Plouhinec.

Near Plouhinec, there lies a barren stretch of moor where only coarse grass grows, and the yellow broom of Brittany. On this plain stand the stones of Plouhinec, two long rows of them.

On the edge of the moor lived a farmer with his sister Rozennik. Rozennik was young and pretty, and she had many suitors, yet she saved her smiles for Bernez, a poor lad who worked on her brother's farm; but the farmer refused to consider Bernez as a suitor until he could show him his pockets full of gold.

One Christmas Eve, while the farmer was feasting his men, there came a knock on the door, and outside in the cold wind stood an old beggar who asked for shelter for the night. He looked a sly, artful old rogue, but because it was Christmas Eve, he was made welcome and given a place by the fire. After supper the farmer took him out to the

74

stable and said that he might sleep there, on a pile of straw. In the stable were the ox who drew the farmer's plough and the donkey who carried to market whatever the farmer had to sell.

The beggar was just falling asleep when midnight struck, and, as everyone knows, at midnight on Christmas Eve all the beasts in a stable can speak to each other, in memory of that first Christmas in the stable at Bethlehem.

"It is a cold night," said the donkey.

As soon as the beggar heard the donkey speak, he pretended to be asleep and snoring, but he kept very wide awake.

"No colder," replied the ox, "than it will be on New Year's Eve when the stones of Plouhinec go down to the river to drink and leave their treasure uncovered. Only once in every hundred years that comes to pass." The ox looked at the beggar, snoring on the straw. "If this old man knew what we know, he would be off, seven nights from now, to fill his pockets from the kerions' hoard."

"Small good would it do him," said the donkey, "unless he carried a bunch of crowsfoot and a five-leaved trefoil. Without those plants, the stones would crush him when they returned."

"Even the crowsfoot and the five-leaved trefoil would not be enough," said the ox, "for whoever takes the treasure must offer in exchange a Christian soul or the stolen treasure will turn to dust. And though a man may easily find crowsfoot, and he may, if he searches long enough, find a five-leaved trefoil, where will he find a Christian man willing to die for him?"

"That is true enough," agreed the donkey; and the two beasts went on to talk of other matters.

But the beggar had heard enough. He was away from the farm at first light, and for six days he searched the countryside for crowsfoot and trefoil. He found the crowsfoot soon enough, and he found trefoil, but none with more than three leaves; until on the last day of the old year, he found a five-leaved trefoil. Eagerly he hurried back to the moor.

But he found someone there before him. Young Bernez had brought his midday meal of bread and cheese to eat beneath the largest of the stones, and he was spending the few spare minutes that remained before he had to return to work carving a cross upon the stone.

"What are you doing?" asked the old beggar, who recognized him as one of the men from the farmhouse where he had spent Christmas Eve.

Bernez smiled. "This holy sign may be of help to someone one day. It is as good a way as any of passing an idle moment, to carve a cross on a stone."

"That is so," replied the beggar; but while he was speaking he was remembering the look in Bernez' eyes as he watched Rozennik at the feasting on Christmas Eve, and a cunning thought came into his head. "What would you do," he asked, "if you had your pockets full of gold?"

"Why," said Bernez, "I would go to the farmer and ask for Rozennik for my wife. He would not refuse me then."

The beggar leant his head close to Bernez. "I can tell you how to fill your pockets with gold, and a sack or two besides."

And he told Bernez what he had learnt from the ox and the ass; all save how a bunch of crowsfoot and a five-leaved trefoil were necessary if one was not to be crushed by the stones, and how a Christian soul must be offered in exchange for the gold. When he had finished, Bernez' eyes shone and he clasped the old man's hand.

"You are a good friend indeed, to share your good fortune with me. I will meet you here before midnight." He finished carving his cross and

76

ran back to work; whilst the beggar chuckled to himself at how easily he had found someone to die in exchange for the gold.

Before midnight they were waiting together, Bernez and the beggar, hidden behind a clump of broom in the darkness. No sooner had midnight struck than there was a noise as of a great thundering, the ground shook, and the huge stones heaved themselves out of the earth and began to move down to the river. "Now!" cried the beggar. They ran and looked into the pits where the stones had stood, and there, at the bottom of each pit, was a heap of treasure. The beggar opened the sacks he had brought with him and began to fill them hastily; but Bernez, his heart full of the thought of Rozennik, filled only his pockets with the gold.

It seemed no more than a moment later that the earth began to tremble again and the ground echoed as though to the tramp of a giant army marching. The stones, having drunk from the river, were

returning to their places. Bernez cried out in horror as he saw them loom out of the darkness. "Quickly, quickly, or we shall be crushed to death!" But the old beggar laughed and held up his bunch of crowsfoot and his five-leaved trefoil. "Not I," he said, "for I have these to protect me. But you are lost, and it is as well for me, since unless a Christian soul is given in exchange, my treasure will crumble away in the morning."

With terror, Bernez saw that he had spoken the truth, for the first of the stones moved aside when it reached the beggar, and after it the other stones passed on either side of him, leaving him untouched as they came near to Bernez.

The young man was too afraid to try to escape. He covered his face when he saw the largest stone of all bear down on him. But above the very spot where Bernez crouched, trembling, the stone paused, towering over him as though to protect him, while all the other stones had to move aside and pass him by. And when Bernez dared to look up, he saw that the stone which sheltered him was the stone upon which he had carved a cross.

Not until all the other stones were in their places did it move on to where its own pit showed dark, with the shining treasure at the bottom. On its way it overtook the beggar, stumbling along with his heavy sacks of gold. He heard it come after him and held out the bunch of crowsfoot and the five-leaved trefoil. But because of the cross carved upon it, the magic herbs had no longer any power over the stone, and it went blindly on, crushing the old beggar beneath it. And it passed on to its own place and settled into the earth again until another hundred years should have gone by. Bernez ran back to the farm as fast as his legs could carry him; and when, in the morning, he showed his pockets full of gold, the farmer did not refuse to give him his sister. And as for Rozennik, she did not say no, for she would have had him anyway, had the choice rested with her.

78

THE OXEN

Christmas Eve, and twelve of the clock.
"Now they are all on their knees,"
An elder said, as we sat in a flock,
By the embers in fireside ease.

We pictured the meek mild creatures, where
They dwelt in their strawy pen,
Nor did it occur to one of us there
To doubt they were kneeling then.

So fair a fancy few would weave
In these years! Yet, I feel
If someone said, on Christmas Eve,
"Come; see the oxen kneel

"In the lonely barton by yonder coomb,
Our childhood used to know,"
I should go with him in the gloom,
Hoping it might be so.

THOMAS HARDY

THE ROCKING CAROL

Little Jesus, sweetly sleep, do not stir;
We will lend you a coat of fur,
    We will rock you, rock you, rock you,
    We will rock you, rock you, rock you:
See the fur to keep you warm,
Snugly round your tiny form.

Mary's little baby sleep, sweetly sleep,
Sleep in comfort, slumber deep;
    We will rock you, rock you, rock you,
    We will rock you, rock you, rock you:
We will serve you all we can,
Darling, darling little man.

79

BABOUSHKA

Once upon a time, there was an old woman called Baboushka who lived all alone in a little house deep in the forest. She was always busy cooking, cleaning or sewing, and as she worked she would sing to herself. She sang old songs and new songs, and even songs she made up; for it could be lonely in the forest and Baboushka liked to keep herself cheerful. The main road was far away and there were few visitors to the little house, so she was very surprised one winter afternoon to hear loud noises coming towards her through the trees.

"Perhaps it's a bear!" she thought, and trembled. But no, a bear wouldn't crunch through the snow like that. She listened again. Tramp, tramp, tramp. She must have visitors! At once Baboushka ran into the house and put some more logs on the fire. She set the big, black kettle on the hob. A few minutes later, there was a loud knock on the door. Baboushka jumped.

"Who is it?" she called in a scared little voice.

"We are travellers," came the reply. "We are very tired and have lost our way. Can you help us?"

"Come in," cried Baboushka, and she flung open the door. "You are welcome to rest by my fire on this bitter day." A young man came in, smiling gratefully, and leading an older man. Then a third followed, shaking the thick snow from his coat. All three wore rich clothes, and the man who came last had shining gold rings in his ears.

While Baboushka busied herself heating a thick soup and cutting bread, the travellers told her they were journeying in search of a baby prince. "His star was guiding us," they explained, "but the sky is so full of snow that we can't see it any more."

"Don't worry," said Baboushka helpfully. "When you've eaten and rested, I'll show you where the road is, and then you won't need to follow a star!"

"You are very kind," answered the youngest man, "but only the star leads to the Christ child."

Baboushka was astonished. "A child and a star! What can this mean?"

The three men told her that the star was the sign of a holy child's birth and they showed her the rich presents they were taking to him. When she saw them, Baboushka's kind heart rejoiced.

"I wish I could see this child," she murmured.

"Come with us," they cried, "and help us in our search!"

But Baboushka shook her head sadly, thinking that she was much too old to travel, and began ladling out the soup. And when the three men had eaten and rested, they thanked her and set off again through the trees.

The house seemed empty when they had gone, as Baboushka sat rocking slowly in her chair. "I would so like to see the baby prince," she whispered over and over again. Suddenly she jumped to her feet. "And I will! I'll join the search . . . there's nothing to stop me. I'll go tomorrow, so I will!"

Quickly, Baboushka packed a small bundle of clothes, and then she collected together her greatest treasures to take to the holy child: a carved wooden horse, a little cloth ball, an old doll, a few painted fir cones and some pretty feathers she'd found in the forest.

Early the next morning, she wrapped up warmly and left her little house. She tried to find the path the travellers had taken, but fresh snow had covered their tracks.

"Have three kings passed this way?" she asked a farmer.

"Kings! In this weather? What a foolish question," roared the farmer, and he stomped away crossly. Then she met a shepherd.

"Have you seen a bright star?" she asked him eagerly.

"Thousands, old woman," he chuckled. "Right above you. And they all shine brightly!"

A herdsman trudged past with his herd of cattle.

"Have any baby princes been born here lately?" Baboushka questioned him anxiously.

"We've plenty of babies," he replied, "but not a prince among them."

She tramped on wearily, stopping everyone she met to ask, "Have you seen the Christ-child, please?" but no one could help her.

And to this very day, Baboushka has never stopped searching; she still travels her country looking for the baby prince. And whenever she meets with a child who is sick or unhappy, she digs deep into her pack and always finds a little toy to make them smile.

THE THREE DROVERS
an Australian poem

Across the plains one Christmas night
Three drovers riding blithe and gay,
Looked up and saw a starry light
More radiant than the Milky Way,
And on their hearts such wonder fell,
They sang with joy, "Noel! Noel!
Noel! Noel! Noel!"

The air was dry with summer heat,
And smoke was on the yellow moon;
But from the heavens, faint and sweet,
Came floating down a wond'rous tune;
And as they heard, they sang full well,
Those drovers three, "Noel! Noel!
Noel! Noel! Noel!"

The black swans flew across the sky,
The wild dog called across the plain,
The starry lustre blazed on high,
Still echoed on the heavenly strain;
And still they sang "Noel! Noel!"
Those drovers three, "Noel! Noel!
Noel! Noel! Noel!"

JOHN WHEELER

WE THREE KINGS

We three kings of Orient are;
Bearing gifts we traverse afar,
Field and fountain, moor and mountain,
Following yonder star.

O star of wonder, star of night,
Star with royal beauty bright,
Westward leading, still proceeding,
Guide us to thy perfect light.

Melchior:
　　Born a king on Bethlehem plain,
　　Gold I bring, to crown him again,
　　King forever, ceasing never,
　　Over us all to reign.

Caspar:
　　Frankincense to offer have I,
　　Incense owns a deity nigh;
　　Prayer and praising, all men raising,
　　Worship him, God most high.

Balthazar:
　　Myrrh is mine; its bitter perfume
　　Breathes a life of gathering gloom;
　　Sorrowing, sighing, bleeding, dying,
　　Sealed in the stone-cold tomb.

All:
　　Glorious now behold him arise,
　　King and God and sacrifice,
　　Alleluia, alleluia,
　　Earth to the heav'ns replies.

THE CHRISTMAS STORY

EVERY year Christian children all over the world look forward to Christmas, the birthday of a little boy called Jesus who was born almost two thousand years ago. This is the story of how it happened.

All those years ago, there was a young girl who lived in the little town of Nazareth in Palestine. It was arranged that this young girl, whose name was Mary, was to marry Joseph, a carpenter who lived in the same town. But one day, as Mary was sitting alone, a light more brilliant than the sun suddenly streamed down on her from the sky. In terror, Mary shielded her face, but a voice spoke gently through the light and comforted her.

"Do not be afraid, Mary, for you have found favour with God." Slowly she uncovered her eyes. Before her stood the angel Gabriel, come as a messenger from God. And this was the message that he brought:

"Behold, you will bear a son, and you shall call him Jesus. He will be the Saviour of all people and king for ever and ever." With these words, the angel left Mary, and the brilliant light faded.

Some months later, when Mary's baby was almost due, a ruling went out through the land where Mary and Joseph lived. The Roman

emperor ordered all the men of that country to go back to the place where they were born to be counted, as he wanted to know exactly how many people lived in the land.

Now Joseph was a descendant of the great king David, and came from David's city, Bethlehem. So Joseph the carpenter and Mary his wife set off for Bethlehem, which was several days' journey from Nazareth. Mary sat on their little donkey, while Joseph trudged wearily by her side. At last, one day towards evening, they saw the lights of the city ahead and their hearts lifted. But when they reached the darkened streets of Bethlehem, they found that many people had come

from far and wide to be counted, and everywhere was crowded. "No room! Sorry, we have no room!" people said at every house and every inn.

The last place they came to was a small inn on the edge of the city.

"No room!" called the innkeeper, but then he noticed Mary's pale face and saw how tired the couple looked. "But if you don't mind sharing with my animals, there's plenty of clean straw in the stable over there, and the ox and ass are gentle creatures and will keep you warm."

That night Jesus was born. There was no cradle so Mary wrapped him in swaddling clothes and laid him in a manger used by the cattle.

Through the same cold night, shepherds were guarding their sheep on the hillsides beyond the city. Suddenly, right above their heads, the sky shone with blinding light, and a messenger from God appeared before the frightened shepherds.

"Do not be afraid," said the angel, "for I bring you tidings of great joy. Tonight the Saviour of the world is born. Go to Bethlehem, the city of David, where you will find the baby lying in a manger." And then the air was filled with the sound of angels singing the first carol:

Glory to God in the highest
And peace to his people on earth.

The shepherds were silent as the beautiful light faded. Then they whispered to one another,

"Let us go and find the Saviour of the world."

They left their sheep and ran down to Bethlehem, where they found Mary and Joseph in the stable, and the baby sleeping in the manger. The shepherds knelt down and worshipped him, happy that the angel's words were true. Then they left the warm light of the stable and hurried through the dark town to tell everyone they met of the wonders they had seen.

89

O LITTLE TOWN OF BETHLEHEM

O little town of Bethlehem,
　　How still we see thee lie!
Above thy deep and dreamless sleep
　　The silent stars go by.
Yet in thy dark streets shineth
　　The everlasting light;
The hopes and fears of all the years
　　Are met in thee tonight.

O morning stars, together
　　Proclaim the holy birth,
And praises sing to God the King,
　　And peace to men on earth;
For Christ is born of Mary;
　　And, gathered all above,
While mortals sleep, the angels keep
　　Their watch of wondrous love.

How silently, how silently,
　　The wondrous gift is giv'n!
So God imparts to human hearts
　　The blessings of his heav'n.
No ear may hear his coming;
　　But in this world of sin,
Where meek souls will receive him, still
　　The dear Christ enters in.

THE TWELVE DAYS OF CHRISTMAS

The first day of Christmas
My true love sent to me
A partridge in a pear-tree.

The second day of Christmas
My true love sent to me
Two turtle-doves
And a partridge in a pear-tree.

The third day of Christmas
My true love sent to me
Three French hens,
Two turtle-doves
And a partridge in a pear-tree.

The fourth day of Christmas
My true love sent to me
Four colly birds,
Three French hens,

Two turtle-doves
And a partridge in a pear-tree.

The fifth day of Christmas
My true love sent to me
Five gold rings,
Four colly birds,
Three French hens,
Two turtle-doves
And a partridge in a pear-tree.

The sixth day of Christmas
My true love sent to me
Six geese a-laying,
Five gold rings,
Four colly birds,
Three French hens,
Two turtle-doves
And a partridge in a pear-tree.

The seventh day of Christmas
My true love sent to me
Seven swans a-swimming,
Six geese a-laying,
Five gold rings,
Four colly birds,
Three French hens,
Two turtle-doves
And a partridge in a pear-tree.

The eighth day of Christmas
My true love sent to me
Eight maids a-milking,
Seven swans a-swimming,
Six geese a-laying,
Five gold rings,
Four colly birds,
Three French hens,
Two turtle-doves
And a partridge in a pear-tree.

The ninth day of Christmas
My true love sent to me
Nine drummers drumming,
Eight maids a-milking,
Seven swans a-swimming,
Six geese a-laying,
Five gold rings,
Four colly birds,
Three French hens,
Two turtle-doves
And a partridge in a pear-tree.

The tenth day of Christmas
My true love sent to me
Ten pipers piping,
Nine drummers drumming,
Eight maids a-milking,
Seven swans a-swimming,
Six geese a-laying,
Five gold rings,

Four colly birds,
Three French hens,
Two turtle-doves
And a partridge in a pear-tree.

The eleventh day of Christmas
My true love sent to me
Eleven ladies dancing,
Ten pipers piping,
Nine drummers drumming,
Eight maids a-milking,
Seven swans a-swimming,
Six geese a-laying,
Five gold rings,
Four colly birds,
Three French hens,
Two turtle-doves
And a partridge in a pear-tree.

The twelfth day of Christmas
My true love sent to me
Twelve lords a-leaping,
Eleven ladies dancing,
Ten pipers piping,
Nine drummers drumming,
Eight maids a-milking,
Seven swans a-swimming,
Six geese a-laying,
Five gold rings,
Four colly birds,
Three French hens,
Two turtle-doves
And a partridge in a pear-tree.